Second Sight

For the very talented Karen! I hope

11/12/21

Second Sight

Poems by

Rosemary Royston

You enjoy! much love & health to you —

Cover design by Shay Culligan

ISBN: 978-1-63980-040-7

Kelsay Books
502 South 1040 East, A-119
American Fork, Utah 84003
Kelsaybooks.com

Acknowledgments

82 Review: "I have never understood," "The Shape of Love," "Place d'Armes"

Accents: "Lessons"

Appalachian Review: "Prunus avium," "On a Dark Road"

Drafthorse: "Mirror Image," "The Way It Is"

Echoes Across the Blue Ridge: "Dogwood Winter"

Fried Chicken and Coffee: "Greasy Creek"

FutureCycle Press: "Pathology"

Gyroscope: "Ars Poetica"

Kudzu: "Mountain Hoodoo"

Mom Egg Review: "What the Granny Woman Knows"

Mom Writers' Literary Magazine: "Conversation(s) during the ride home from primary school"

Mountains Piled Upon Mountains: Appalachian Nature Writing in the Anthropocene: "Haint How To," "Broom Lore," "Magickal Substitution," "Apis Mellifera"

Museum of Americana: "Appalachian Superstitions as Told to the Poet," "Appalachian Ghazal"

POEM: "Acer rubrum"

Poetry South: "Ezra's House"

Public Republic: "On the Discovery of Aspirin"

Snake Nation Review: "Grocery List"

Southern Poetry Review: "Where I'm From"

Split Rock Review: "Rumex acetosella"

Switchgrass Review: "Caretaker," "Type 1"

STILL: The Journal: "Oxydendrum arboretum"

The Rose in the World: "First Nightmare"

Town Creek Poetry: "Reasons to Go Outside at 4:58 am in November"

Vitamin ZZZ: "Magickal Remedies for Acute Insomnia"

Deep gratitude to those who've come before me and shared their wisdom, specifically Edain McCoy, H. Byron Ballard, Nancy Richmond, and Misty Murray Walkup. This collection would not exist without them and others who've shared their stories with me.

Contents

III Second Sight

IV Blue Hills

Ars Poetica

after Jackson Wheeler

Because Mom was from New York and Dad from Oklahoma.
Because of the Doxology and slender, brown hymnals. Because of
forests I wandered solo. Because *Gone with the Wind*. Because of
covered-dish meals on granite tables. Because of summers in
Rockland County. Because of my transistor radio and Marvin
Gaye. Because of the guy in 10th grade and the front of his daddy's
Caprice Classic. Because I memorized *The Gettysburg Address* and
A Child's Garden of Verses. Because of S.E. Hinton. Because he
was innocent and no one believed him. Because *nothing gold can
stay*. Because of soil and squash and radishes and fig trees.
Because of what lies at the bottom of the lake.

I

Mountain Hoodoo

What the Granny Woman Knows

With anything that's born th' mothers have t'suffer,
Mrs. Echols, *Foxfire 2*

Even so, to cut a hemorrhage
slide an axe, blade up,
under the bed. For fever,
a bowl of water.

A sharp knife under the pillow
is rumored to slice pain
to tolerable bits. To ease delivery,
sip nettle. To bring on labor, rue.

Carry bloodstone in the left pocket
or have your partner draw a talisman
on your belly during a new moon
to ward off miscarriage.

Never, ever, spin wool, knit,
or leave anything knotted
in the house of the mother,
or the umbilical cord may strangle.

Babies born with a caul are gifted.
Dry and preserve the caul, mix with herbs
for a healing potion, keep pieces
in a locket or small bag for protection.

Mountain Hoodoo

after H. Byron Ballard

i.

Unnatural bleeding? Whisper Ezekiel
16:6 three times: *Live! Yes, I said to you*
while you were in your blood,
and the bleeding shall cease.

ii.

Enemies? Plant a stob
in the ground to set a boundary
and push back your oppressor

or, write their name
on a raw egg. Bind it
with yarn, cover
the shell. Place in the freezer
for a moon cycle, then toss
into a running stream.

iii.

Warts? Notch a small branch
with a knife for each wart.
Wrap in a dirty dishrag
and bury. Wait a full moon
to be wart-free.

iv.

To draw out fire? Move your hand
across the burn. Repeat,
There came an angel from the east
bringing fire and frost. In frost, out fire.

v.

The gift. After her first cycle,
a young woman's powers
appear. She'll see the future,
hear the words
of lingering spirits.

Appalachian Superstitions

A menstruating woman should never
                make kraut
                be near cucumbers,
                be near mash
                or attempt canning.

A menstruating woman should
                study with a Granny Woman,
                whose powers are abundant.

A woman who buys dreams
                must avoid purchasing
                the nightmares of children.

A man who has never seen his father
                can cure thrush
                by blowing into an infant's mouth.

For faster growing hair, have it cut
                by a pregnant woman,
                or during the full moon.

Cows should be kept
                in odd numbers
                or the herd will grow ill.

Keep pigs around for luck
                but don't pull their tails.

Hares out at night:
                servants of the devil.
                Hares out in day:
                food.

Harassing a cat is the same as
                    harassing the local witch.
                    Don't.

Spiders are servants of God.
                    To wake to a newly spun web:
                    Exceptionally good luck.

Appalachian Ghazal

A bird flies through the front door:
death in the family.

A raven rests on your rooftop:
within a fortnight, death in the family.

A blackbird perches on the windowsill,
caws, takes a trinket: death in the family.

A rooster or hen crows at midnight:
death in the neighborhood.

An owl (*Satan!*) flies over your home—
death.

A dog howls three times in a row, after dark.
Death, but to whom?

Stand behind the beast, gaze over his head.
Suspended there, between his ears,

the face of one soon to pass.

Magickal Substitution

i.

Bring a shovel into the house
and a grave will be dug by December.

Rest a tool against the interior wall,
illness will manifest in death.

To defeat the spell, break the shovel
or tool in half. Bury in separate places.

ii.

If you're hit by a falling rock
pieces of your soul will escape like fog.

Take the rock and find two others
similar size, shape, color.

Cast the three stones into a stream
in the name of *the Father, the Son,*

the Holy Ghost. Or, instead,
Maiden, Mother, Crone.

iii.

A blackbird perches on your windowsill,
caws its ragged caw. Death is near.

You must kill the bird after it takes flight.
Burn it, bury its ashes at the edge of the cemetery.

iv.

The crowing hen or rooster after dark?
Kill it, too. Wipe its blood on the doorpost.

v.

If a white dog stops and gazes upon you
in the setting sun, the only way to save your life:
drink a tea brewed with the dog's drool.

Magickal Remedies for Acute Insomnia

after Edain McCoy

Dear B—

I'm sorry you're having trouble sleeping.
I'm visiting Aunt Edain. Here's
what she says to try:

Soak the bark from a black locust or birch tree
in pig urine and place under your mattress.

Sleep with your head at the foot of your bed.

Spend the night at Old Union cemetery,
aligned in the same direction as the dead.

Drink milk from an eggshell.

Sip a tea of boneset leaves.

Repeat (any above) every Sunday 'til cured.

Much Love,
R—

In the Name of

She worked in the financial aid office,
trusted only numbers until
her infant boy could not heal from the thrush,

white blisters in his mouth. Fussy,
refusing to nurse, losing weight. Nothing
the pediatrician offered helped,

so she gave in. Loaded the baby,
drove down Old Blue Ridge Highway
to Mulky Gap (she once pointed out

the house to me—it was blue,
swayed in the strongest wind).
The elderly man inside

had never seen his father,
was known for curing the thrush.
He took Baby T from her,

walked into his bedroom, whispering,
I do this in the name of...
The next morning: the thrush was gone.

Disappeared, she said. *Vanished.*

Primer for a Southern Appalachian Healer

Collected from Richmond and Walkup's Appalachian Folklore

Belladonna treats the bite of a rabid dog,
boneset deters an unwanted suitor.

Clove and marigold deflect gossip,
celandine ends an argument.

Cowslip relieves migraines, vertigo,
steers away uninvited guests.

Fennel wards off mosquitos and enemies,
fenugreek attracts money.

Toss crushed lobelia into the air to calm a storm,
use St. Joseph's Wort to ensure fidelity.

Solomon's Seal keeps the ghosts away,
rue repels fleas and pesky werewolves.

Broom Lore

Never loan your broom,
as brooms take an interest
in their home. When you move, leave
your broom behind. If you allow
another's broom into your house,
you invite disaster.

Nothing evil can cross a prone broomstick,
so lay one lengthwise across the hearth
to stop wicked things
from slinking down the chimney.

Brooms are guardians,
keeping out the evil. Sweep at least
once a day, but steer clear
of the feet of an unmarried woman,
or she'll be a spinster forever.

Wedding Ring Divination

For a simple *yes* or *no*
ask your question
roll the ring in front of you—
If the ring breaks left: *no*
If the ring breaks right: *yes.*

For a complex question,
make a pendulum by attaching the ring
to a strand of hair. Suspend.
When the ring is still, inquire.
If the ring moves
from right to left: *Stop.*
Up & down: *Things are good.*
Corner to corner: *unseen influences*
at play. Switches direction: *danger.*

Divining

The husband scoffs when I inquire
on the mystery of dowsing,
says there is a science behind it,

explains why the forked limb
vibrates when encountering water.
Which may just be this: there's water

everywhere underground. Maybe divining
is luck. Even so, I find lessons
from a man in Sylva, NC, who crafts

dowsing rods, has a *how to* on his site.
I can now dowse not just for water,
but also lost objects.
He recommends I practice alone

or with a skilled dowser.
Before searching, ask: *May I?*
Can I? Should I?
Never to misuse the gift.

Haint How To

After dark, avoid
      narrow woodland trails,
      the base of dead trees,
      wherever lightning has struck,
      and (obviously) graveyards.

To keep the haints away,
      hang basil over the threshold,
      plant rue or purslane near your home,
      spin three times, counter-clockwise,
      before entering the house,
      hang chimes on the front door.

To banish haints
      at sundown, offer the ghost a snack
      of raw potato. At dawn,
      bury the potato, and your ghost
      will be grounded, never to return.

II

Healing Salve

The Shape of Love

Mother was beautiful until she was not. It was the 70s. I don't
think it was the brown, polka-dot polyester dress. It was, instead,
my exit from Eden. Waking into reality. I saw Mother's strong jaw,
her determined cheekbones. But there was a violent halo of sun
around her face. Pock-marked skin. Coffee breath. Scream-cries of
new brother.

I hid that day. In a large brown box that came from *babushka*. I hid
and the parishioners looked and the police in that small red-dirt
town were called. Search. Searching. I'm asleep. In the box. The
smell of packing tape and grandma's house.

Love is distant and comes in the form of a cube. You have to
unwrap it. Sometimes you have to use a knife or sharp scissors to
cut through the tape and string. Be careful. The blade will surely
slip.

Emory Hospital, 1975

The floor shines like ice and looks as slick.
The man in the bed next to yours has a tube—

like you—that weaves through his chest
and empties into a jar. The liquid is green—

he chewed grass for years until a fungus grew
and his lung collapsed. Just like yours, Daddy.

It felt like a fish hook
pulled with a sudden piercing tug.

Your scar runs from nipple to spine—
a pink smirk.

And I, your daughter,
am tossed into dark waters

with no line.

Lesson

His patience was thin
as a sheer curtain; his resolve,
steel. My freedom hinged on learning
to drive the family stick-shift
that humid June afternoon.

I could only pop the clutch
and in his rage he swung at me,
his left arm a mallet.

This was my father, who kicked
the cat and threw a Bible out a moving
car. Until then, he never struck me.
I countered with the slam of the door
when the Toyota finally choked.

There he remained
frozen in the passenger seat,
the one with the cigarette burns,
staring blankly into an empty horizon.

Greasy Creek

The house was built, years ago, with large,
smooth stones from the creek that snaked
through a patch of river cane.
So much energy went to the outside
that the floor joists gave way long before
they should've. For three months I lived there
with J and C, man and wife. My upstairs room,
a windowed alcove with racks of clothes
and a transistor radio. No cells, no TV.
For entertainment we had skunkweed,
a porch swing and books.
Once a month the pump broke,
leaving us grimy and irritable.
I earned my keep pulling lettuce, spinach,
squash, cooking biscuits from scratch.
Me with my silly make-up bag and hairdryer,
C with her clear skin and braided mane.
We sat on the porch, talked about building
a greenhouse, which never got further
than a dark womb in the earth.
On weekends people appeared—
C's brothers and sisters, or E, the neighbor
with the yard of cars. He was 50, yet had
the body of a knife-carrying teen.
His wife, pregnant and smoking, silent.
On Sundays, after everyone wandered
off, C opened the windows
while the sun danced over the scratched
wood and C's voice filled the room.
I followed her to the center of myself,
oblivious to the sinking floor,
the wasps nesting in the corner of the ceiling.

Eve and the Apple

Can you imagine
the first crunch?
Did Eve hold the apple to the sun,
turning it slowly
before she bit?
Did her tongue flick out
to catch the juice
that ran past her lips?

How the sweetness
coupled with the shock
of her bare thighs and breasts
must have made her run to Adam,
the apple in her outstretched hand
as she choked on the urge to confess.

Can you see his face
as concern and puzzlement turn
to fascination? I ask you,
is it not the same now
as then:
how we relish
in the sweet
red taste of sin.

Ezra's House

The hardwoods were paint splattered,
Pollock-like. The former owner, Ezra,
left his mark in this 40s bungalow
off a dirt road that overlooked a pasture
lined with Queen Anne's lace.

The first year asparagus grew on its own.
Snapdragons and marigolds filled sagging
window boxes, and we left the windows open
until first frost.

Inside, I painted brown panel white,
the trim mint, and ignored the orange shag.
I turned the avocado fridge
glossy white with appliance paint.
My husband patched holes in the bedroom.

We never forgot that first weekend,
a baptism of sorts,
as we unloaded box after box,
the radio loud—
how the DJ announced *Better Than Ezra,*
but instead of the song:
a buzz, silence. The power flickering off
as Ezra's name hit the air.

Retinitis

Grandfather Pawlicki stared at the sun,
told it would strengthen his eyes.

As a child he hid his eyes as his father
chased his mother around the kitchen table
with a butcher's knife.

When I visited him and Nanny P in Pearl River,
NY, he'd sneak religious tracts into my suitcase.
He broke Nanny's heart by leaving the Methodist Church

for the Radio Church of God, which opened his
bulging blue eyes to the alleged lies of vaccinations,
the scam of fluoride. Legally blind, he taught

me to drive in his burnt-orange work truck,
gear shift on the column. His breath smelled
of St. Pauli Girl, and he kept beer in the attic

until he brought it down to the fridge.
Before I was of age, he introduced me to anisette,
the licorice-like liqueur burned my nose and throat.

He couldn't see the cigarette butts my husband tossed
in the kitchen trash, but he did smell them,
and demanded they be thrown elsewhere.

I never understood Grandpa P. I was somewhat
frightened of him until one visit I witnessed
him holding my daughter, both of them scooted

close to the small TV watching Jimmy Sturr
& His Orchestra, Gpa's foot tapping to the polka music,
my daughter in his lap, nibbling a cookie.

I have never understood

naps. How long do they last? 15 or 20 minutes? Two hours? Tell a mother with a colicky baby what a nap is. My mother took one nap. The next day she had a hysterectomy. If my children see me napping, they worry. Mommy doesn't nap. Naps are for cats. I'd rather sleep 12 hours straight than have a 30-minute nap here, an hour there. Unless we're talking Sunday "naps." The kind mother and father took after lunch, their bedroom locked. When I leaned close to the door, I could hear their hymns, sung in unison, through breath and tongue.

Conversation(s) on the ride home from primary school

What if the only food in the world was
spaghetti?

What if it rained pickles?

What if it rained pennies? *You'd need a stronger
umbrella!*

What if there was a tree *(were)*

that grew dollars and you could only *Where are the results
from my
mammogram?*

pick a dollar if you were going to *How will I pay
save the dollar and every time the painters?*

you did this another one would *When will they be
done?*

grow back? *What in the world
will we have for
supper?*

Spaghetti.

Removal

It'll sting, he says.
The first one does. Shots
two and three even more so.
Though I'm numb, I feel
the pressure of hands and scalpel
as the mole comes out—
the one larger
than a pencil eraser,
asymmetrical,
varied in color,
that resides—*resided*—
over my right breast.
The pony-tailed doctor,
who's donned a pair of glasses,
is gentle as can be
but I still cringe and click
the toes of my black boots together
as he threads the needle
through my chest—
three stitches
for the ladybug of flesh
that is now suspended
in a vial of clear fluid.

Pathology

Diagnosis: *Nevoid Lentigo.*
A lentiginous proliferation
of melanocytes is present,
occasional small nevus nests
in the center.

Translation: Benign.

Imagination: A proliferation
of tiny birds once nested
above my right breast.
The beat of their wings
over-ridden by the beat of my heart.
Their dark nesting spot
sometimes slipping out
of the top of my blouse.
Once an identifying mark,
now an extinct species. I miss
the flutter of wings. I miss strolling
with birds in my chest,
their occasional songs
now scarred shut.

My uterus says no

to the thin tube whose goal
is to extract a slice of endometrial tissue.
This is not a surprise, my uterus

has said *no* before. *Remember that other
failed biopsy attempt?* I say.
But the ob/gyn pays no mind. She

props open my cervix to gain entry
into an uncooperative uterus. *No.* My uterus,
unconcerned about minimal spotting,

is not interested in offering a sample.
The doctor and I are determined.
Tell me a story! I blurt, and up from the stirrups

floats: *My husband was bitten
by a rabid raccoon while fishing yesterday.*
No way! I say, briefly distracted

before my scream of pain erupts.
The doctor shakes her head,
I can't torture you like this. She pulls

out the tube and speculum while I wipe
tears, wondering how many shots
are required for a rabies bite, and what

one does when her uterus
defies entry, the lining continually
thickening, unyielding.

Sterile

After anesthesia there will be vomiting.
Your son rubs your back
as you once rubbed his.

The pre-op instructions stated
no shaving two weeks prior, yet you wake
naked in your nether parts.

You try to recall the minutes before the IV,
the kind nurse who hugged you,
the moments after. Time bends,

disappears. The heart attack
you think you're having? Gas.
Take comfort in that. And once

you've emptied your bladder,
you're free to leave,
cauterized
and glued shut.

On the Discovery of Aspirin

Could it have been a three-day headache—
the kind with the relentless throb and slam
of the sledgehammer, the sick roll of the eyes,
the ache in the base of the neck,
that drove someone into the woods
shrieking in two parts pain, one part delirium
just mad enough to rip off slender leaves
and shove them into his mouth, the bitter taste
bringing relief not long after,
> or was it the midwife, helpless
against the feverish flesh and moan
of the laboring woman, who ran into the dusk,
tearing bark from a tree while reciting a prayer
in some unknown language, later helping
the baby make its way into the world
as the mother's skin cooled and she wept
softly, like a willow bending in the breeze.

Grocery List

When mother visits she writes
a grocery list. Her neat script
is cheerful in its curves,
but bold in its weight,
for on the sheet underneath
is a shadow of all she writes.

Not just olive oil
Extra virgin olive oil—
the kind her new friend
from New York
(whom she met at church
while I was sleeping)
uses in her own pasta salad
(the one with walnuts).

This is the kind of olive oil I need.
I may not know this.
I may not know to make a list
for groceries, or would
forget to buy
the brand her friend uses,
so, she has underlined
the brand name right next
to the words *Extra virgin*
on my grocery list
in my kitchen.

Caretaker

for BW

He says he's in his 60s. His body: granite. He has the stance of a
young man who'll never grow a midlife softness. Jeans, work
boots, his shirt unbuttoned low, the edges of his cut off sleeves
sewn as not to fray. A gold cross hangs against his brown chest. He
leans against the railing of the deck he built this year. Feet crossed,
arms crossed. He looks me in the eye when he speaks. He's been
on this mountain since he was ten. His daddy—the caretaker
first—now him. When the college got the land, he came with it.
*Hell, who else knows where the water lines are, the gas lines,
anyway?* The only map is in the coarseness of his hands.

He checks on me just short of noon with a loud knock. I'm busy,
but he will appear later, his white sideburns wings under his Chevy
hat. The tattoo I didn't see yesterday now evident. Right bicep, a
cross. Faded red. He never says her name but he tells me how he
cared for his wife. Pancreatic cancer. Doctor got it wrong; thought
it was her stomach and then it was too late. How she refused him
when he said she needed a hospital bed. *They don't make 'em for
two.* So he didn't get one until he had to, until he was afraid she
would break when he lifted her. He moved his bureau and gun
cabinet out of the bedroom, pushed his bed as close to hers as he
could. He says he never wants to feel that kind of pain again. We
look across to the ridge, below us the steep drop off where the
leaves are twenty shades of green.

For That Time When I May No Longer Recall Myself

I keep my onions in a bowl marked FRUIT.

My default is to leave a drawer open.

I share my sink with a speck of a spider,
and refuse to wash it down.

The art of napping
has always escaped me.

I prefer Audubon to Betty Crocker.

When I visit the park, I opt for
the skate court over the basketball court.

A phone ring scares me
as much as a fire alarm.

I misplace my bras,
which I rarely wash. I don't buy white.

I keep a Bible on the bookshelf,
but never open it.

Place d'Armes

What should I have done
in Jackson Square
but eat beignets and sip coffee?
I did what I was afraid to,
allowed a woman with long red hair
to read my fortune. She turned the tarot
slowly, looking at me, then back at the cards.
The wind blew and colorful glass
held down the cards.

You're an empath, she announced.
I thought everyone
was like me: their radio frequencies
jammed with the feelings of others
unaware of what belonged to whom.
Her eyes grew soft.
She advised baths in Epsom Salts
to release emotions I carried,
watch them circle down the drain.
She gave me a blue stone,
that now sits on my dresser,
its coolness a healing salve.

The Way It Is

You stand in line at CVS in shoes
pinching your feet after eight hours.
Everyone else's prescription is there
but yours. You spend sixty-eight dollars
for groceries, dodge puppy shit
baking in the gravel drive
lug in milk, cereal, ground beef.

Above, the sky is grayish-blue.
The sky is gray.
The sky is blue.

You fill a Mason jar with a zinnia,
purple wildflowers whose name
you do not know, and a fern
picked from down by the pond
beside the carpet of green moss
where, whenever you pass,
you sit, remove your shoes,
and reverently rub the soles
of your feet.

Reasons to Go Outside at 4:58 am in November

Because it is more silent than you can imagine
the moon a nickel
glinting off the unseen sun,
surrounded by broken crystals.

The limbs of bare trees
webbed arteries,
under a sky whose shade
has yet to be named.

There, you will find your mouth agape,
eyes lifted, knees
sinking into the fallow garden,
praying, regardless of belief.

Mirror Image

Even the Baptist minister's wife is dressed
like me today: short shorts, bikini top, brown skin

though it's early spring. Both of us know
when to plant bulbs, how to till,

when to move the seedings into the soft brown.
This morning I braided my shower-wet hair,

hers is coiffed from church, but we're both
in our garden spot with a hoe and rake.

Our repetitive motions mirror one another,
as do the echoes of the *clink* of metal on stone.

We make the rows even and straight
and rake weeds and debris to the edge.

We stop to rest, lean against the padded handle,
look across our yards, lift a hand in *hello*.

Where I'm From

after George Ella Lyon

Always a state line nearby, a lake, pine trees.
Border towns with only one or two traffic lights
full of people who know each other

from grade school through their senior year,
who live with two generations on plots of land
with cows, chickens, or turkeys, where kids drive

four-wheelers or stick-shifts by the age of 10,
towns with names like Elberton, Lincolnton,
and Inman, where my family and I were given

a brick ranch-style parsonage with pea-green
living room sets, a slab of concrete for a patio,
a garden spot. I'd know the people of those small

places for five years, at most. Sunday services
at Coldwater, Cokesbury, or New Bethel Methodist.
Covered-dish dinners outside, granite headstones

nearby. Every pew had brown hymnals, pencil stubs
for pledge cards. I'd sing the *Doxology,* kneel
for communion. Surrounded by people, I pretended

to join in prayer. But what I loved was the softness
of soil when my bare feet sank into the freshly tilled
garden and, as I grew braver, the woods,

climbing trees and disappearing into webs and clouds.

Variations on a Favorite

after William Carlos Williams

i.

I drink desire
as if it were water,

eat hearts whole,
pits, rinds, and all.

Forgive me, I am weak
but so very bold.

ii.

I devour the earth
swallow seeds and soil,

sprout flowers from my fingertips,
petals from my wrists.

I guzzle cool streams
flowing with rose hips.

iii.

I am the leaf
that's ever green

in summer's sweat
and through winter's ache.

I am lover to each. My roots
know no regret.

Salve

When sound hurts,
when desire is a rock,
and when darkness leaks from every pore,

the only cure is to bathe
in the light of moon.
Undress. Shed all that's artificial.

Lie on the ground under the pine,
on the moss by the pond,
or in the middle of a field.

Feel the air on your flesh,
how parts rarely exposed
tingle. You smile. You recall

an act you have long forgotten.
Do not move. Stay.
This is prayer.

III

Second Sight

The Knowing

The gift of second sight, that, as a child,
I longed for—
How I wished for it,
again, that February of near-death:

Not a virus.
Not leukemia.
Not mono.
Not anything

the doctor could diagnose, until the ER,
after weeks of fruity breath, chest pains,
random vomiting,
the (secret) bedwetting—

my emaciated boy
an IV in his neck
and the sick realization I knew,
I'd known, all along, that something
was wrong.

Type 1

Insulin smells like band aids. Or maybe I should say like adhesive. I don't know which. When I gave my son his first shot, all I could think was, *insulin smells like band aids*. How do band aids smell? Open a box and put one on.

Physical shock has many manifestations. Such as leaning over a toilet in the ER and throwing up. Hearing a buzz in your ears that isn't really there. Standing only to feel the small room spin, while being sickened by the overpowering smell of industrial soap. To leave your body, shift from *woman-in-crisis* to *mother-in-charge* and breathe like a yogi master. To hold your son's dry hand as nurses search for a vein.

February. A month of specificities: the nurses in the PICU with their endless supply of scrubs (magenta, turquoise, orange prints with blue bears); how it's important to remove the bubble in the syringe before the injection; how the chicken fingers in the hospital dining hall taste as good as homemade when you know your boy is going to be okay.

Even now, though, when I say my son has an autoimmune disease, I feel the center of my being sway, as if on a rope bridge. We think *the center will not hold*. But it can. It smells like band aids.

Sudden Awareness of Embodying the Dialectical

Brian was a pale child. I was his 13-year old
babysitter. An unexpected snow, and we broke
the rules, snuck under the barbed wire,
slushed towards the iced-over pond
moving too close to something we knew
nothing about. Suddenly, he slid down the slope,
broke the thin ice with a pop. I bolted
to pull him out, nearly didn't connect
both of us reaching, eyes as black as the water.

Second

I'm the sitter, sitting for the surreal:
Scott's stepfather stabbed to death
by an escaped convict who hid in a dark corner.
My summer was spent with Scott—
cooking canned lunches, playing games.
Then I watched this child who had witnessed
such horror. *He'll feel comfortable with you,*
his mother said as she left for the funeral.
Scott and I looked blankly at one another,
no words, no games, only shock
lurking in the corners with its persistent, silent howl.

Third

I sat on Ronnie's lap in the backseat
on the way to a basketball game,
his hands on my legs, my waist, inching upward.
That was the last time I saw him alive.
At the viewing, I realized his lips were glued shut,

his hair sprayed in place. Later, I visited the junkyard
to stare sickly at his RX7. A summer breeze blew.
There were crushed beer cans.
The car had collapsed into itself
a twisted maroon accordion.

Fourth

My son, 13. Me, his father, his sister,
clueless. It was February.
The month now conjures cold hospitals,
diabetic ketoacidosis,
a crash course on using a syringe,
counting carbs. And the glucagon pen
in case he slips into a coma.
So many numbers. Desired range: 80-180.
Prick at least three times a day.
Check now.
Will he wake up?
Check again.
Is he high or low?
The darkness is always there,
hovering, with its glued-shut mouth.

Mother's Apparition

She slept on the scratchy couch
in her grandparents' den.
It was 1947. As she napped,
she dreamed of an elegant doll—
not one for play,
but a formal one, porcelain,
brought all the way from Russia
when her grandparents immigrated.

When she woke, she crossed the street
to play with a boy
whose mother allowed them—
just this one time—to climb the attic stairs.
Mother's skin crawled,
the hairs on her arms raised,
as she gazed at the same doll of her dream,
its exquisite gown
even more elaborate in waking life.

On a Dark Road

Slow down, I said,
I, barely a teen, holding that man's child,
a man I thought I loved,
love being the most misguided word,
love neither what he did nor gave.
He drove down a dark, twisting road
surrounded by pines
Slow down.
You're going to hit a deer.
His look of irritation
slung towards me like a slap,
the sweat of his son's flesh against mine
the slam of the brakes,
the busted headlight, broken mirror,
a head against the windowpane.

First Nightmare

after Ronald Lockett's painting, Holocaust

Here it is, my first nightmare,
imprisoned on the canvas:
skeletons clustered in the dark.
In *my* dream, a cave,
in Lockett's, a boxcar, captured in paint.

He was inspired by *Escape from Sobibor,*
I'd just read *The Diary of Anne Frank.*

Tucking me in, Mother told me
it was real, not make-believe.
I felt the breath go out of me,
the nausea rise.

Then the nightmare
of the fleshless bodies
in the dark and airless cave.

IV

Blue Hills

Oxydendrum arboreum

I never seen bees go crazy like they do on sourwood,
Foxfire 2

Lily of the Valley tree
Leaves, long and glossy
dark green in summer, scarlet in fall.
Chew but don't swallow,
to quench your thirst.

Best bee tree
Your flowers are angel fingers,
bees flock to you, buzz.
Your honey is the long sweetening kind
not the short of sorghum.

Sorrell tree
Acidic soil, shallow roots
curved trunks
to shape into tool handles, bed posts.
Cut a limb the height of an asthmatic
child, and place the limb under the doorstep.
Once the child outgrows the limb,
the asthma will disappear.

Prunus avium

Graceful eating it is not—
you must have muscle, desire
an adroit tongue that twists

and slides the pit to one side
as teeth separate sweet meat.
Do you spit

before or after summer
explodes in your mouth?
The contemplative

strips the pit of every flesh-bit
until smooth as a river stone
while fingertips seek

the firmest in the bowl
ever thankful for the fleshy drupe
and its staining juice.

Dogwood Winter

Ants raid the bath, wasps claim the washroom,
even as the cool of winter looms.

The forsythia sings against a chorus
of green, yet the hue of winter looms.

The bunting's a blur of vibrant blue,
off-setting winter's gray loom.

Calves nurse in the open field, chilled
as the nip of winter looms.

Blood buds of azaleas burst forth,
even though winter looms.

The creek hums a rain-filled song
oblivious to the winter that looms.

Rosemary, thyme, and sage grow
in the sunroom, even as winter looms.

Urtica dioica

She'll sting you—don't be fooled
by her heart-shaped leaves,

her abundance. Play safe.
Wear gloves to harvest,

soak her in water to neutralize
the prickle. Her list of healing powers

is long: she kills intestinal worms,
prevents osteoporosis, cures bladder

infections, repels fleas.
Her leaves are filled with protein.

She pulls the sting from a bee.
Sipping a tea of her dried leaves

will ease a baby's delivery.

Apis mellifera

Benevolent bee, who only stings
the dirty or wicked. Beloved bee

who spins liquid gold, while looking after
the pure of heart. I plant lemon balm, borage,

as invitation. I tell you of a family death
or you will leave and die yourself.

You gather at your keeper's gravesite—
a stop along the way to your new home.

I am grateful for you, your sourwood honey—
which, with moonshine, helps all possible ails

here in the blue hills of God.

Rumex acetosella

No thought was given to what it really was,
poisonous or not, Allison just called it *sourgrass,*

plucked the leggy plant with its reddish top,
sucked it like a straw. The opposite of honeysuckle—

bitter, like olive brine. My mouth watered.
I liked it. That summer we ransacked it from pasture,

backyard, roadside ditch, far from discriminate.
It flourished in that Piedmont town, where granite

headstones and mausoleums were always on display.
Here in the mountains I rarely see it, so I research it,

red dock, sour dock, common sheep sorrel just three
of its names. Edible, with a love of acidic soil,

host to the American Copper, to young girls
who saunter outdoors, brave enough to eat weeds.

Acer rubrum

Naked, next to the storm door, he motions me over,
points to the blazing red maple.

When his long limbs graze mine, my flesh
turns as scarlet as the maple's leaves.

I want to stay on this mountain for at least
as long as it takes each crimson leaf to fall,

to twist to the ground like a mariachi
dancer in *rojo:* the color of love, the color of lust,

the color of the pomegranate, of blood,
this brilliant burgundy of Autumn's maples.

When I leave, the word *goodbye* singes
my tongue, burns my rose-colored mouth.

This collection would not be possible without the following:

The Orchard Keeper's Residency, and those who helped shape this collection into its final form: Bethann Bowman, Jason Lee Edwards, Elizabeth Glass, Denton Loving, and Eric Sheranko.

Source materials:

Appalachian Folklore: Omens, Signs, and Superstitions, Nancy Richmond & Misty Murray Walkup

Folk Medicine in Southern Appalachia, Anthony Cavender

Mountain Magick: Folk Wisdom from the Heart of Appalachia, Edain McCoy

The Foxfire Book and The Foxfire Book 2, Eliot Wigginton

Staubs and Ditchwater: A Friendly and Useful Introduction to Hillfolks' Hoodoo, H. Byron Ballard

Those who shared superstitions and stories:

Lori Baker
Mary Cooper
Donna Crow
Shea Daniels
Kayli Dixson
Ruby Dixson
Mary Jo Dyre
Jason Lee Edwards
Jane Hicks
Karen McElmurray
Mike Milsaps
Vicky Milsaps
Amy Partin
Mary Ricketson
Darla Wilson
Sylvia Woods

About the Author

Rosemary Royston resides in the northeast Georgia mountains with her family. Her writing has been published in journals such as *Appalachian Review, POEM, Split Rock Review, Southern Poetry Review, STILL: The Journal, Poetry South,* and **82 Review.* Her photography has been published in *A Rose in the World, Bloodroot,* and *New Southerner.* She is an Assistant Professor of English at Young Harris College.